MARSHWOOD VALE

The Complete Dorset Poems

by

David Bushrod

With illustrations

by

Roger St. Barbe

Copyright 1995 David Bushrod (Text)
Roger St. Barbe (Illustrations)

First Published November 1995
Second Edition April 1997
Expanded Edition September 2002
Fourth Edition December 2007

ISBN 978 0 9542678 0 3

Not to be resold in any other form.

Published by D. Bushrod, 34 West Allington, Bridport, Dorset DT6 5BQ

Printed by Creeds the Printers, Broadoak, Bridport, Dorset DT6 5NL

NOTE

This edition of Marshwood Vale includes all the poems previously published as *Abbotsbury: Songs of the Abbey Lands*.

CONTENTS

PLATES

Snowdrops

MARSHWOOD VALE

The simple beauty that the world disdains
Enfolds the Dorset countryside I know,
But wander down these quiet embroidered lanes
Where meadowsweet and wild viburnum grow.

No mountains here, no tumbling waterfall
Whose thunder echoes round some craggy vale:
A tourist spectacle complete with all
The gaudy splendour of a peacock's tail.

Here nothing wilder than a dimpling stream
Disturbs our peace: a place where life is worth
The living, and where human lives can seem
Still woven through the fabric of the earth.

SNOWDROPS

White hoar-frost still enshrouds this leaden scene,
But soon the little beaks of muted green
Now breaking through the fertile earth will bring,
The first of all the flowers that bloom in Spring:
And when the dainty pendent bells unfold
We'll glimpse the tiny stamens drenched in gold.

ST. CATHERINE'S CHAPEL

More like a fortress than a saintly shrine
With massive walls and solid barrel vault,
Was it perhaps by an inspired design
Built to withstand the infidel's assault?

Long since abandoned on this windswept hill,
Like some proud outcast now it stands alone,
Defending with indomitable will
Something more precious than the crumbling stone.

For rosaries of fervent prayer have left
A presence here by which the heart is stirred:
Though lonely, desecrated and bereft,
The echo of our faith can still be heard.

MARCH 5TH

Wild daffodils I found today, and narcissi
Of coolest jade and ivory
And knew that Spring would come.

So now the woods I comb
For signs that Summer will appear,
And flush with radiant hues, this world of bleak despair.

THE BLACKTHORN YEAR

For Spring the reckless blackthorn cannot wait
But strews her blossom on the frosty air,
And long before the warblers first appear
She clothes herself in chaste unearthly white.

Such fragile flowers to meet so dark a fate,
And yet the Summer's growth will soon betray
The virgin promise of their infancy,
And sour the Autumn with much bitter fruit.

And then when Winter comes and cold winds moan
Through hedgerows where night-haunting barn owls screech,
The branches, crooked, gnarled and sharp, will stretch
Like witch's fingers up towards the moon.

SPRING FLOWERS

In memory the primrose does not fade,
And bluebells trailing in the wake of Spring
Will still reflect the azure sky, and bring
A golden vision of some woodland glade.

But in reality the beauty of the land
Is tainted with the odour of decay,
And Time erodes the things we love away,
Remorseless as the tide upon the strand.

THE LILIES OF THE FLEET

With simple majesty the white swans float
Like precious lilies round the water's edge,
And strew the beauty of a vanished age
Across the tranquil surface of the Fleet.

How Leda would have loved and Jove despaired
Amongst this blossoming of swans:
For Leda would have found a dozen swains
Before great feathered Jupiter appeared.

SONG

The leaves in Spring when first unfurled
Are subtle pristine shades,
But loose amongst this wayward world
With wanton haste their vernal beauty fades.

Could man from this world's acrid stain
His innocence uphold,
Or like the trees his youth regain
And with each Spring fresh leaves of faith unfold.

The Lilies of the Fleet

5

THE ABBEY RUINS

How few the traces that remain
Of all the Abbey's wealth today:
But all the works of man contain
The fertile essence of decay.

And yet we seek stability:
Though nothing earthly seems to last,
Like ivy round a withered tree
We cling to fragments of the past.

BUTTERFLY ORCHIDS

Last year about the evening woods I found
A drift of orchids: luminous and white,
They stood like votive candles all around
And shone resplendent in the fading light.

This year I searched the lonely woods again
And heard the cuckoo and the blackcap sing,
But sought for orchids on the ground in vain:
Exotic flowers are faithless to the Spring.

So next year I shall search the woods I know
For bluebells and the crane's bill stained with wine,
Tall foxgloves and the primroses that grow
In festive clumps beneath the eglantine.

THE WHITE HART

A white hart watched me in the woods today:
Something there was about his haughty glance,
A hint of sorcery and dark romance,
He stared at me and proudly stalked away.

His antler tips were burnished like a crown
And on his coat there was a regal sheen.
I smiled to think that in these woods I'd seen
An ancient beast of fabulous renown.

I felt transported to a different age
To watch a hunting party pass my way,
With hawks and hounds and knights in rich array,
And highborn ladies with a negro page.

COWSLIPS

I hate the bloated hyacinths that grow
In pompous ranks about the town.
Can anything that gardeners ever sow
Compare with cowslips on the open down?

Like sunlit clouds on Walditch hill they stand
Bending so sweetly in the winds caress,
They bring true beauty to this ravaged land
And wake the frigid heart to tenderness.

Spring Woods

SPRING WOODS

Each Spring for nearly threescore years
I've wandered in the kindling woods,
And felt the beauty of the flowers
Was far beyond the reach of words.

For words are but the breath of man,
Weak, inarticulate and vain,
Whilst even simple flowers remain
Expressions of a power divine.

POWERSTOCK FIELDS

Rare are the colours and the scents
That butterflies entice
Who float, on angels wings, above
These fields of paradise.
And rarer still the nectar served
In cups of sunlit gold,
Far sweeter than the finest wine
By any vintner sold.
But do the butterflies recall
A life of weary grind,
When they were tied to solid earth
Like hapless humankind?
And do the caterpillars know
When leaves grow thin and stale,
That they will slip like magic through
A metamorphic veil?

THE ELDER REPLIES

O rampant vulgar humpback of the hedge!
What right have you to flourish there?
And with rank growth engulf the Summer air
Where dainty blossoms seek earth's skyward edge.

'One equal right have all however pure,
One obligation too however strong;
Whoe'er you are, whoe'er you live among
They are the same: to struggle and endure.'

THE WILD ROSE

Of innocence and purity
The Rose of England speaks,
For maiden virtue blushes through
Her petals pink as cheeks.

A sense of innate mystery
Inspired by ancient laws:
A fragrance sweet, but reticent,
And thorns as sharp as claws.

The Wild Rose

ABBOTSBURY

Here where the Abbey chancel stood
The light of faith once shone,
And one must feel a certain guilt
For honest grandeur gone.
From France the Benedictines came
On weary blistered feet,
And no doubt thought they were secure
In this remote retreat.
They built; they tilled the soil; they bred
The swans that grace the fleet.
They led a life which must have seemed
Both blessed and complete.
For centuries a life unchanged:
Like bees inside a hive
With varied, patient industry
They laboured to survive.
The dissolution was abrupt.
That grim satanic deed,
That act of crafty sacrilege
By Christians was decreed.
Like jackals with a still warm corpse
They broke the Abbey's bones,
Then picked the carcase clean and built
This village with the stones.
Four hundred years have now elapsed
Since those events occurred,
Or since the bells last woke the night
And matins last were heard.

What happened to the roofless monks?
The men of faith betrayed!
Was any sympathy expressed
Or any shame displayed?
Even God would not defend the monks
Against the wrath of kings,
Though Chesil Bank defends the Fleet
And cloistered calm still brings.
The swans still congregate and breed:
Their purity and grace
Are such that they have now become
The icons of this place.
Sacred, serene, and free to roam
Where once the brothers trod,
Protected by the hand of man
If not the hand of God.

IN PACE REQUIESCAT

Just like the shards of faith that can be found
Entombed amongst the debris in the mind,
Cadaverous beneath this narrow mound
The Abbey's old foundations lie confined.

Dusk

LINES

Like light from stars a thousand years expired
Your beauty still illuminates my life,
Untouched by Time or marred by useless strife
Your face seems still by innocence inspired.

DUSK

Dusk seeps across the vale:
As darkness dawns the radiant colours die,
  And then the night creates
A photographic negative of day.
  A magpie world in which
The strange and the familiar seem wed.
  On silent ghostly wings,
The nightjar haunts the margin of the wood,
  And in the shapeless gloom
About the moonlit heath, the badger stirs,
  And fiery glow-worms ape
The distant beauty of the twinkling stars.

REMEMBRANCE DAY

I can remember when the poppies grew
In scarlet drifts about the shepherd's folds,
But nothing beautiful will ever grow
In all these sullen weed infested fields.

Shall we forget in future barren years,
That where the nettles and the ragwort stand,
There bloomed, in other years, much finer flowers,
And once these fields with richer hues were stained.

THE SUMMER WOODS

Spring passes like a storm, and her
Fecundity subsides:
But life still burgeons in the woods,
For though the bluebell tides
Have ebbed, the foxglove spires stand high
About the wandering rides.
The nightingale is mute, but still I hear
Across some murmuring glade,
The soft monotony of doves
Half drowsing in the shade.
But Summer days will soon be gone
And Summer flowers will fade:
For even now, when night winds cause
A tremor in the fir,
And from the tangled undergrowth
The ghostly nightjars churr,
I feel within the sleepless woods
The breath of Winter stir.

SONNET

That burning sweet intensity that sears
The youthful heart with passionate desires,
Ambitious dreams and vague uncertain fears,
Now seems but ash from long forgotten fires.

Will any worthwhile vestige still remain
Of all the ardent hopes that once were mine?
Or have Life's petty burdens been in vain
And once bright flowers died fruitless on the vine?

For as the wasting years slip past, I find
Hints of the trouble that the abbots found:
That Time and savage circumstances grind
Even great monuments to level ground.

What drives us on or lures us from afar
Who neither wisdom have nor guiding star?

SONG

Now I have tried the path that winds
Across the barren moor,
And felt the chiding of the winds
That all the seasons mar.

So I shall leave the lonely wold
And go where hidden paths reveal,
A verdant loving sunlit world
Within the sheltered vale.

LEWESDON HILL

The ancient woods on Lewesdon Hill
Are paradise to me,
For under Summer skies I find
Profound serenity.
But does the beauty draw me here
That all this place pervades?
Or does some Siren spirit haunt
These unfrequented glades?
The beauty here is manifest:
The restless sighing trees,
And view across the sunken vale
Of distant sparkling seas;
The scent of woodbine; wild brier rose;
And fresh unsullied dawn;
The glory of the dappled light
That hides the sleeping fawn.
But spirits too seem still to drift
About this sacred place,
Of Marshwood men who tilled the soil
But left no earthly trace,
And when my spirit shall be free
To wander like the breeze,
I think that it will settle too
Like mist about these trees.

Lewesdon Hill

HARVEST SONG

With joy the work of Spring was done,
The fields were raked and sown:
We caught the breaking of the dawn
And darkness came too soon.

All Summer's beauty now unfolds
With life the meadows seethe,
And soon we'll hear across the fields
The whetstone on the scythe.

KINGSTON RUSSELL STONE CIRCLE

Fallen these stones and long since lost the creed,
But still they form a bridge through Time and seem
The fossil record of an ancient dream,
For which men died and human hearts still bleed.

But all creeds die, no truth is quite secure:
However much the priests may scheme and plan
Beliefs are mortal as the flesh of man,
Though like these stones the bones of faith endure.

THE RELIC

Now cradled in this cottage wall
And tightly clasped lest it should fall;
Protected from the world's alarms;
An infant held in loving arms
This shard of sculpted Abbey stone.
Did someone think they could atone
For that malign unholy act
By saving just one artefact?
One fragment of a shattered world,
Still finely chiselled, crisp and curled,
Which from its pulpit seems to say
'You once had faith but not today.'

THE RAVENS

Deep in the shadows of the pine
The ravens build their nest,
And there where moonlight does not shine
Like Charon take their rest.
Though safe, they feel Death's presence near,
They listen as the night wind sighs
And from the wood's dark heart they hear
Such bitter, anguished cries.
At dawn they leave their gloomy perch,
And stretching wide their quills,
The Stygian undertakers search
For carrion on the hills.

THE ABBEY LANDS

They built a glorious Abbey here to pray
For God's protection in a savage land.
How could those trusting monks now understand
This awful desecration and decay?

The hallowed relics of the past are tossed
With casual abandon all around,
And now this land where once such peace was found
Looks like a battlefield when hope is lost.

Only the undefeated chapel stands
And like a grim crusader holds its ground:
As though by some quaint pledge of honour bound
Still faithful to the haunted Abbey lands.

Eggardon

NIGHTFALL ON EGGARDON

From heaven now the lark descends and folds
Her young beneath her breast,
And as the colours of the afterglow
Fade slowly in the west
A strange expectant hush pervades the land:
No wind to stir the listless harebells there;
No sound but bat's wings beating in the air.
Come closer now beloved: take my hand:
Eternity will wait for us amidst
The stillness of the night,
So let us taste Life's sweetest rapture by
The moon's exquisite light.

THE SPIRIT OF THE VALE

Beneath the wrinkled brow of Eggardon
Like braided nets the fields stretch far away.
A land of firm tradition still, where one
May find the ancient yoke in use today.

Old customs, old beliefs are often best,
So let the rustic spirit of this land
Defend us with the greatest strength and zest,
From every speck of progress that is planned.

23

SUMMER'S LEASE

Spring set our love alight,
And I recall
It glowed all Summer long
Like burning coal.

You were so beautiful,
Your face so pale,
I thought my love for you
Would never pall.

But then the withered leaves
Of Autumn fell,
And like a frost nipped bud
My love did fail.

GOLDEN CAP

These cliffs, the earth's decaying memory,
Intrigue us with the thought of past epochs,
And as we search among the scattered rocks
For fossils from some long quiescent sea,
Sweet memories of youth and lost content,
Just stir beneath the dross that fills the mind,
And gleam awhile like ammonites we find
Washed clean among the sand and sediment.

EPIGRAMS

The silver birch is trembling into leaf:
We sense the burgeoning of life
And Spring is here, is here.

The Summer broods are growing fast: no dearth
Of aught save thoughts of lonely death:
Of Winter frosts no fear.

The fading countryside is dank and moist:
The trees peep through the Autumn mist
That shrouds the dying year.

And Winter comes: in troubled times we note
The stars that twinkle in the night
When skies are clear, are clear.

THE ANCIENT THORN

On Blackdown hill there stands a threadbare thorn,
So old that few can still believe it lives.
Even in June its foliage is so thin
It seems to have more lichen than green leaves.

But now in Winter when the leaves have gone,
Haggard and gaunt, its end at last seems nigh,
And yet I know that it will bloom again
Thicker with flowers than all these fields with snow.

25

Chapel Woods

26

CHAPEL WOODS

Here in these old decaying woods
The chapel's ruined arch,
Though long abandoned, still impedes
Time's brisk destructive march.
And some think too that in these woods
A spirit still abides,
Remote, mysterious, aloof,
Unquenched by human tides.
Elusive as the Holy Grail,
But which to senses keen,
Just like the fragrant woodbine makes
Its presence felt unseen.
I feel it in the pregnant hush
That awed me as a boy,
But now uplifts my aching heart
With ecstasy and joy:
And when among the woods I sense
This pure tranquillity
Then something deep within me stirs
In mystic harmony.
This world recedes, horizons dim,
Life's complex burdens slip,
As though my heart was safe at last
In Time's eternal grip.

BUZZARDS

Their stronghold is the sky: above
The vale they soar like Fates.
Evil: ever-circling: they move
And Destiny dictates.
Like Nemesis they watch the world
Through hooded, downcast eyes.
They note where rabbits stray
Too far from cover, and where lies
The timid leveret concealed
And take them by surprise.
This part of God's exquisite plan
May seem to human eyes,
The perfect symbol to reflect
The agony and strife,
The merciless brutality
That darkens earthly life.
Below the landscape looks sublime,
No outward sign of stress
Betrays a doubt of inner peace
Or perfect happiness.
On Hardown Hill the blackbird sings
With tranquil, careless ease,
And cowslips on the open ground
Flirt lightly with the breeze.

NOVEMBER

November and the frosty woods
Have rashly shed their Summer cloak.
Such folly that a simple clerk
Can find no apt descriptive words.

And yet when April comes again
The reckless woods will still revive,
And with fresh ecstasy and verve
Unfold a rustling silken gown.

WINTER WINDS

The toadstools thrive about the rusty woods;
When Autumn comes they never fail,
Though other plants decay and fall,
And all the world is dressed in widows weeds.

And like a nest when all the young have flown
The woods are desolate and bare:
The trees, like mourners round a bier,
Forgotten stand, despondent and forlorn.

'Come Winter winds and scour the chilly groves
Lest any trace of Summer should remain,
Or one small flower, however mean,
Should comfort give to any heart that grieves.'

QUARRY HILL

On Quarry Hill they dug the stone
To build the Abbey in the vale,
And let the breath of ages stain
The crumbling lichen covered shale.

I quarried deep within my mind
For gems as permanent as jade,
But only built a little mound
Of chippings of the lowest grade.

I wandered in the Summer woods
With ill-starred hopes of lasting fame,
As though my simple rustic words
Could brand the landscape with my name.

But man and fame are mortal still
And in the evening's fading light,
Like flocks of roosting birds they steal
Into the shadows of the night.

THE WAYWARD GORSE

Deep lies the snow about the withered bracken
And rough winds bend the branches of the pine.
All, all is frozen still and Summer's sleep unbroken.

But leave the vale and go where voices beckon,
High on the windy slopes of Pilsdon Pen,
For there the wayward gorse is flowering like a beacon.

David Bushrod was born in 1938. He grew up mainly in Wiltshire and the Isle of Wight but has lived most of his adult life in Dorset. He studied literature for his degree and as well as the poems in this collection he has written poetry about Wales, humorous and nostalgic essays, and the *libretti* for two operas *The Devil's Trill* and *Echo and Narcissus*. Both of these have music by Brian Parkhurst who has also composed two song cycles based on a selection of these poems.

Roger St Barbe has been making etchings for 25 years. He came orginally from London but in 1990 moved to Colyton where he has his own gallery. His subjects include landscapes of Devon, Dorset and Cornwall, as well as wild flowers. He has exhibited widely and his work has been shown at the Royal Academy. The technique he uses

involves acid etching on metal plates, aquatint (a form of tonal etching), and finally hand-colouring with watercolour.

Musical settings of poems, and hand coloured originals of plates in this book can be obtained through the following websites:

www.mostynmusic.com
www.dolphinhousegallery.co.uk